Written by Catherine Allison
Illustrated by Iris Deppe

First published 2016 by Parragon Books, Ltd.
Copyright © 2019 Cottage Door Press, LLC
5005 Newport Drive, Rolling Meadows, Illinois 60008
All Rights Reserved

10 9 8 7 6 5 4 3 2 1

ISBN 978-1-68052-551-9

Parragon Books is an imprint of Cottage Door Press, LLC.
Parragon Books® and the Parragon® logo are
registered trademarks of Cottage Door Press, LLC.

NOAH'S ARK

PaRragon.

Long, long ago, when the world was still new, God saw that all was not well. Golden sun still warmed the days on Earth, silver moonlight gilded the nights, and the hills, valleys, rivers, and seas were as beautiful as on the day God made them. But the world had changed. The people had become wicked. They fought one another, hurt one another, and made mischief. They had forgotten that God wanted them to be good—in fact, they had forgotten God completely. Seeing this made God so unhappy that He wished He'd never made people. He decided that something must be done.

As God looked down on the world, His eyes fell upon one man, whose name was Noah. Noah was the only man on Earth who remembered God. He worked hard every day, despite the fact that he was very old. His wife, his three sons, and his sons' wives all worked hard, too. They were happy, kind to each other, and good to their neighbors, even though they received no kindness in return. They lived a good life—the sort of life God had hoped all people would live when He created them.

God was pleased with Noah and his family. He decided that they deserved to live on Earth and He would protect them. But everyone else had been wicked, and they could not be saved.

God told Noah about His plan to change the world.

"The world is full of wickedness," God said, "so I am going to send a great flood to wash it clean. Nearly everyone and everything will be wiped away, apart from you and your family, Noah. The world will begin again, as fresh and good as when it was first created, and you and your family will live there."

Noah was very frightened.

"What must I do?" he asked, trembling.

"You should build an ark," said God. "It must be big enough to hold two of every animal in the world—one male and one female—and food for all of them. It must be strong and watertight, because it will be battered by the flood waters for many days."

"I will do exactly as you say," said Noah.

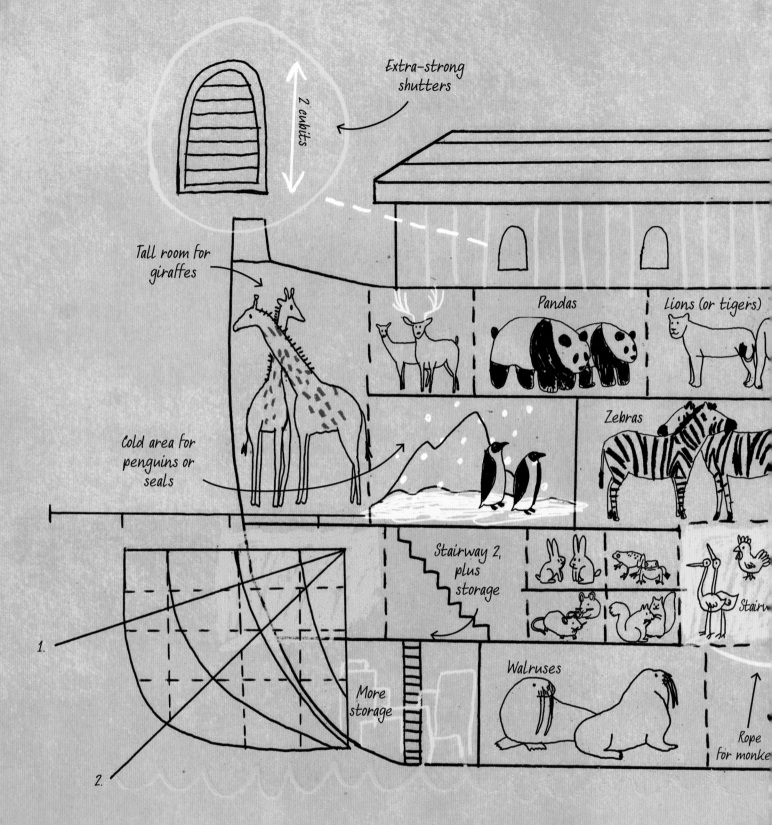

Extra-strong shutters

2 cubits

Tall room for giraffes

Cold area for penguins or seals

1.

2.

Pandas

Lions (or tigers)

Zebras

Stairway 2, plus storage

More storage

Walruses

Stairw

Rope for monke

Noah was glad that he and his family would be saved from the flood, but he was sad about what would happen to the world and all the other people, and worried about what God had told him to do.

"How can I build such an ark? I'm not a shipbuilder," he thought.

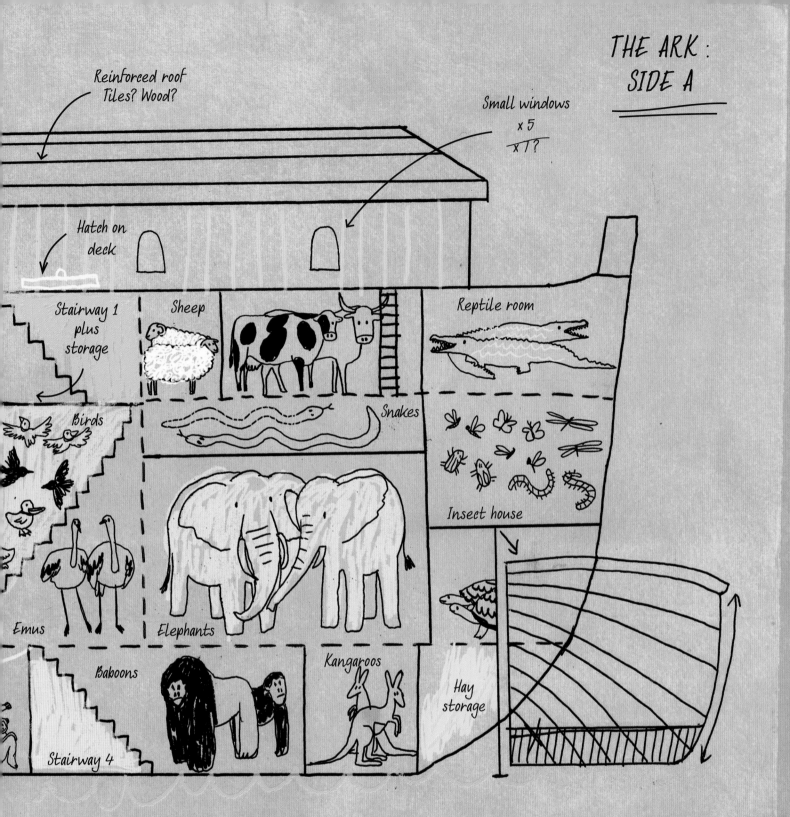

"And how can I collect so many animals? God expects so much of me and I'm afraid I will fail."

But God wouldn't let Noah fail. He was there beside Noah every step of the way, helping him and telling him what to do.

Noah and his sons worked hard, chopping, sawing, sanding, and hammering, and gradually the ark took shape.

While Noah worked, God spoke to him.

"It will rain for forty days and forty nights, and the land will be covered with water. But you, Noah, will be safe in the ark."

As Noah and his sons worked, their neighbors watched from a distance.

"What are you doing, Noah?" they asked, laughing at him. "Why do you need a boat when the sea is miles away?"

Noah heard them laughing, but he took no notice.

After many weeks, the ark was finished. It was taller, longer, and stronger than any boat there had ever been. It was slick, smooth, and shiny on the outside, with strong shutters at the windows and heavy locks on the door—the perfect boat for stormy weather. Inside, there were many rooms, some wide enough for the largest pair of elephants to walk side by side, others high enough for the tallest giraffes to stand in without bending their necks.

All of a sudden, dark clouds appeared in the sky and thunder rumbled. The people who had been laughing at Noah saw that the weather was changing and started to head for home.

"Perhaps Noah isn't such a fool after all," said one. "There's a storm coming for sure, and he'll be safe and dry inside the ark."

Noah began to gather the animals—a male and a female of every creature that hopped, walked, crawled, or flew on Earth. There were cats, bats, and rats, monkeys and donkeys, hooting owls and wolves that howled, big baboons and little raccoons—so many animals, of all shapes and sizes. Noah and his sons led the animals up the gangplank and into the ark as the rain began to fall.

"We don't have much time," thought Noah.

The sky turned black and the rain fell harder.
Noah's wife, his sons, and his sons' wives made
sure all the animals were safely on board, then
they went into the ark. With one last glance at
the world he loved, Noah went inside, too, and
shut the heavy door behind him.

Outside the ark, rain fell everywhere. Not a soft drizzle, but soak-to-the-skin, drench-to-the-bone rain. Raindrops became puddles, and puddles flowed into streams, oozed into lakes, and poured into wild rivers. Then all the rivers joined together and became an angry ocean. The once-dry land was overwhelmed, and hills and homes were gone forever.

Noah and the animals watched through the windows, safe and dry inside their ark.

For forty days and forty nights, it rained. The ark was pulled and pushed, up and down, to and fro on the rainwater ocean. Inside, the animals were frightened and Noah did his best to calm them. He trusted God and knew that all would be well in the end.

At long last, the rain stopped, just as God had said it would, and the ark lay still on the water. Then, strong winds began to blow. Little by little, the water level dropped and the tips of the mountains appeared. The ark came to rest on one of them—a mountain called Ararat. It seemed that the ark's journey was over.

Noah watched from a window, as land continued to appear. Then he sent a raven out into the world to see what it could find. An hour later, it came back tired and worn—and Noah knew there was nowhere for it to land.

A week later, Noah sent out a dove. After some hours, it returned with an olive twig in its beak—and Noah knew it had found at least one tree with branches above the water. It meant that Earth was drying out.

"Not long to wait now," he thought.

After one more week, Noah sent out the dove again. This time, the bird did not return—and Noah knew it had found a dry place to land.

"Now it is safe to leave the ark," he said to his family.

Noah flung open the doors, and the animals filed out of the ark. They raced away in all directions, glad to stretch their legs and run free. The birds flew off to find twigs to build new nests, and the deer trotted off to search for fresh, green grass to eat. The giraffes walked and the lions ran, the monkeys scampered, and the kangaroos hopped. Soon, they would all find new homes and raise their families on the new, dry land.

After all the animals had left the ark, Noah and his family left, too. Noah wanted to thank God, so he built an altar of stones and bowed his head to pray.

"You saved me from the flood and brought me to dry land again," said Noah. "I will always be thankful."

God heard Noah's prayer and was pleased.

"Now is the time for a new beginning on Earth," He said. "I bless you and your family, and I wish you well. You must have lots of children, so the world will be filled with people again. All Earth's riches are yours— the animals and plants, the land, and the seas. They belong to you, and you must take care of them."

"Thank you, God," said Noah.

"One more thing," God continued. "I promise that I will never send another flood to destroy the world. Look up and you will see a sign."

Noah looked up at the sky. The gray storm clouds drifted away and bright rays of sunlight shone for the first time since before the flood. As Noah watched, God made a brilliant rainbow appear, which stretched from one end of Earth to the other.

Then, God spoke again.

"Whenever you see a rainbow in the sky, you will remember this day and my promise to you. Now, Noah, go and begin your new life."

Full of joy and thankfulness, Noah walked down the mountain to join his family and the new beautiful world.

Now, when we see a rainbow in the sky, we remember God's promise to Noah. It's also a promise from God to us and to our beautiful world.